From Welfare to Faring Well

From Welfare to Faring Well

*How We The People Can Eradicate
the Entitlement Mentality & Poverty
that Plagues America*

In Pursuit of the American Dream
A Life Enrichment Book Series #3

Nancy S. Gaskins, Founder
*US Ambassadors for Prosperity
www.iTrainInvestors.com*

US AMBASSADORS
FOR PROSPERITY

 iTrainInvestors.com

Dear

Carpe Diem! (Seize the Day)
TODAY is the <u>first</u> day of the rest of your life!

Remember to live each day as if it's your last;
with NO regrets.
May you always wake up happy and rested,
with a smile on your face,
and go to bed content from your accomplishments
for the day.

~Nancy Gaskins

Dedication
In Honor of My Childhood Friend

Jan Ann Biggs-Combs

My #1 prayer warrior and partner in crime.
My confidant and life-time friend,
through the good, bad, and ugly times.
You have been my greatest cheerleader,
always encouraging me,
reminding me of my gifts and talents.
How could I ever survive without those midnight-thirty
texting sessions that only "we" can understand.
I pray our next 50 years will be better than all the rest.

Love you girlfriend!

Jeremiah 29: 11
Proverbs 3:5-6
Job 8:7

Contents

Part 1 Program Overview

Part 2 The Plan

Part 3 SPONSORS

Prosperity Manifesto 2017

WE THE PEOPLE opt to stand up, join hands, start holding our government, and ALL the freeloaders of society accountable for wasting our hard-earned tax dollars. YOU know who you are; your family knows, and so do your neighbors.

WE THE PEOPLE are making a stand today to put you on notice: "enough is enough." To be clear, we are not referencing the people who genuinely need assistance. We know you're there. We know your struggle is very real; rest assured that better help is on the way.

$712 BILLION dollars of our hard-earned tax dollars was blown on 13 welfare programs in 2015. Government programs may not work, but WE THE PEOPLE, do.

WE BELIEVE in accountability, and giving a hand-UP, rather than a perpetual hand-OUT. We think that just makes good financial and common sense.

INVITATION: For those of you that are sick and tired of being sick and tired. For those of you who know that you are not living up to your full, God-given potential. For those that are truly interested in changing the current trajectory of your lives and the lives of your families for generations to come. For those that are ready to accomplish more in a year than most people will accomplish in a lifetime.

For those that are willing to be held accountable and have the initiative, courage and conviction to hold others accountable for results. We expect nothing but the very best out of ourselves, therefore, we will expect the same from you.

For those that are excited about the possibility of being part of something that is bigger than any of us; a movement so transforming that the ripple effect could be felt world-wide.

For those that are wondering if this project would qualify for a Nobel Peace Prize. After all, we've seen stranger things happen in years past.

If any of these statements resonate with you, or anyone you know, you are cordially invited to join us in our quest.

OUR COMMITMENT:

We will INVEST in ourselves. We will INVEST in one another.

We are committed, focused, and will be relentless when necessary. We will do whatever it takes to provide the inspiration, training and resources needed to ensure that all Ambassadors are properly equipped.

We do this for a profit, and there is absolutely no shame in our game. We live in America. We have the right to life, liberty, and the pursuit of happiness and all those who are willing to do what it takes, part of that American Dream is the POWER TO PROSPER!

The most important part of this initiative is NOT the impact it will have on the world-wide economy or our national economy, which is made up of all the local communities scattered across America.

The fact that the program will pay for itself, has a self-funding mechanism built in to ensure the program endures long after we are all dead and gone, is also, not the most important.

We do expect and demand a return on our investments, into perpetuity. In fact, it's not out of the question to expect our investment returns to increase in value year after year.

The Closest Thing To "UTOPIA"

The most valuable, important, mind-boggling thing for us to witness and experience will be the massive transformation that will occur in the mindsets of all our people.

Our UTOPIA will be a place where we work together to identify and hone our gifts, talents, and skill sets, and use them for their highest purpose.

We will challenge one another to always rise above, in both our personal and professional lives, with no regrets. We will live our lives on purpose.

Carpe Diem (seize the day) will be our theme each day. No more slacking. No more wasting hours, days, months and years not living; just merely breathing, taking up valuable space, without making a meaningful contribution to society and the world.

Ambassadors are mandated to watch out for one another; always looking out for each other's best interests. There is no room for jealousy for we realize there is more than enough success to go around. Should we dare not follow through on our commitments to ourselves and one another, we have given our fellow Ambassadors full permission to not hesitate, and quickly call us out. We will strive to be better, not bitter.

We have a mission statement and creed that will serve as our compass, keeping us focused and on track. We hold one another accountable, and YES, we keep score.

Our personal finances will improve and people will notice. We will build wealth, increase our net worth, and leave a legacy behind that will be remembered for generations to come.

Our lifestyles will change for the better. Our health will improve, due to the lack of stress in our lives and our new healthy habits. Our careers will flourish because "work," will no longer feel like work. It will be our passion.

Philanthropy will no longer be just a word meant for the elite; it will be our normal way of life. We are ordinary people, living extraordinary lives; lives worth talking about.

We will wake up one fine day to realize that we are finally living the life of our dreams. We have created and are living our very own version of the American Dream, which I believe is what life is really all about.

Mission

Create a lifestyle where I will have enough money, time, health and fitness to do what I want, when I want, with those that mean the most.

Commitments

• Pursue an exciting, well balanced life filled with purpose, achievement and financial prosperity, aspiring to live a life of excellence in both my personal and professional life.

• Live my life on purpose each day by investing my time, energy, and resources on things that truly matter.

• Plan my work, and work my plan so that I can achieve my goals and help others to do the same.

• Do what it takes to look and feel fit, and to age well.

• Commit to live a highly successful personal and professional life; one that is pleasing to God, and will inspire others to follow suit.

• Use my gifts, talents, experience, knowledge, skills, abilities, and resources to make a significant difference in the lives of others, thereby impacting my family, friends, neighborhood, workplace, community, nation, and the world, in a positive manner.

Part 1
Program Overview

The Dream

ABOUT

US Ambassadors for Prosperity, LLC is a citizen-led, entrepreneurial initiative that provides incentives and rewards to individuals, businesses and non-profits who are committed to eradicating poverty and increasing prosperity in the US.

The Wealth Building Program has five key focus areas: work, earn, save, spend, protect and invest.

Membership entitles access to free wealth building classes, financial coaching, mentoring and earn-as-you-learn investor training.

Group discounts for personal and professional development training programs and materials will be available based on group demand.

THE CONCEPT

Imagine a nationwide investment club of epic size. Every household, business and non-profit in America is a Member, and every Member participates. We invest in real estate, business ideas, and people. Everyone who participates gets rewarded… extremely well.

Working together, we inspire, educate, reward, and transform lives in communities across America. The impact will be felt world-wide for generations to come.

From Welfare to Faring Well is a prosperity manifesto that outlines how this new citizen-led initiative can eradicate poverty and increase prosperity in every household, business and non-profit in America, in as little as five years.

The concept is sound and is very easy to explain and comprehend. My largest challenge is finding a cost effective, quick way to get the word out quickly to every household, small business and non-profit in America; currently estimated to be **154.9 million.**

I wrote and published this short book to explain the program and give several step by step affordable ideas on how we can quickly fund and implement this program in communities across America… in record time.

My goal is to have a nationwide membership drive only one time per year, for a 30-day period, which would leave the remainder of the year available for building wealth for our members.

There are at least nine options for you, your family, friends, neighbors, business and community to benefit and PROFIT from joining US Ambassadors for Prosperity in 2017.

MEMBERSHIP FEE

The annual membership fee is only $50 for Individuals, (less than $1 per week), $125 for businesses, and $75 for non-profits.

You would be hard pressed to find anyone who legitimately cannot afford to participate. Most families waste more than that each month on non-necessities. I also have built in attractive financial incentives to encourage everyone to help me spread the word.

I pay cold-hard cash every time someone registers as a new member, sponsor, donates a cash gift, or purchases any product or service.

Every time I get paid, someone will earn a commission. Shouldn't that someone be YOU?

The Numbers

There are an estimated **124.6 million** households in America, **28.8 million** small businesses, and **18,500** firms with 500 employees or more. 23 million small businesses with no employees other than the owner, and 5.8 million with paid employees,

(Source: www.sba.com/advocacy/7540/42371)

The National Center for Charitable Statistics (NCCSS) reports that more than **1.5 million** nonprofit organizations are registered in the US. This number includes public charities, private foundations, and other types of nonprofit organizations, including chambers of commerce, fraternal organizations and civic leagues.

SUMMARY

A 5-year plan to fuel, fund and provide free wealth building classes, financial coaching, and affordable earn as you learn investment opportunities for every single household and business in America.

Priority will be given to families who are unemployed and/or on government assistance programs.

With your help, we will inspire, educate, reward, and transform lives in communities across America. The ripple effect will be felt world-wide, for generations to come.

OBJECTIVE

Our objective is to eradicate poverty and increase prosperity in every household in America by providing a hand-UP, rather than a perpetual hand OUT.

This program will provide inspiration, training, tools and resources that every family in America can use to become more prosperous, moving their family forward towards true financial independence, tracking and documenting their milestone progress every step of the way.

THE DETAILS

Each year we conduct a membership drive kickoff for Ambassadors, Investor Trainees, Sponsors, and Training Site locations.

This funding is used to purchase real estate investments in communities across America. The rental income and/or profits generated from the sale of real estate will be used to build a perpetual cash machine that will fund this program year after year.

At the end of each year, Ambassadors receive a *60% thank you reward* for supporting the program.

FREE Wealth Building Program:

Registered Ambassadors are eligible to apply for the free Wealth Building Program and Financial Coaching.

Applications are processed in the order in which they are received, based on funding availability. Applicants will be placed on a waiting list and will be notified when the next available class has been funded and is open for registration.

US Ambassadors for Prosperity, LLC partners with churches, non-profits, and businesses to provide a facility for our live training sessions. Online options will be made available as funding becomes available to do so.

FUNDING

The US government currently spends $712 BILLION PER YEAR of our hard-earned tax dollars on 13 separate welfare programs, not including Medicaid. That equates to $5,714.29 per household, every single year… a real bottomless money pit.

US Ambassadors For Prosperity, LLC can provide a top notch program that will provide financial training, incentives and rewards to families who are <u>committed</u> to eliminating their dependency on government assistance programs; which would mean a $712 billion dollars in tax savings each year.

An investment of $5.4 BILLION dollars…one time, is what it would take to fund this program. That equates to only $43.34 per household.

Does it make sense for us to invest $43.34 ONE TIME to save $5,714.29 per year? Of course it does.

FOCUS AREAS

The Wealth Building Program will be focused on maximizing efforts in these six key areas: **work, earn, save, spend, protect and invest.**

RETURN ON INVESTMENTS

Besides the obvious positive economic impact in communities across America and life changing financial results that have the potential to impact lives for many generations to come…there is even MORE great news!

Unlike government programs, if we meet our membership registration objectives, we will only have to fund this program **one time.**

We will use the initial campaign funds to establish a perpetual cash machine that churns off enough excess cash each year to self-fund the Wealth Building Training Program.

100% Return on Investment (ROI): Sound impossible or a bit outrageous? Every Ambassador is considered an extremely valuable asset and investment. Our primary objective is to help make each one more valuable and prosperous.

Every family that is accepted into the Wealth Building Program is required to sign a contract to "pay it forward," and sponsor another family.

This commitment guarantees us a 100% return on every family investment, which allows us to double our impact each year without further investment capital required.

SHOW ME THE MONEY

Everyone should be very clear up front that this is a citizen-led entrepreneurial initiative, for PROFIT.

Everyone that helps in any way whatsoever, no matter how small or large the contribution, whether it be a donor, sponsor, member, referral partner, paid employee, contractor, student, or volunteer…will be rewarded for their efforts.

The Breakdown

- **Ambassador Membership Registrations** are used to purchase real estate investment properties that will fund the Wealth Building Training program scholarships each year.

- **Investment Club Membership Dues** are used to fund small business startups and purchase real estate investment properties for vacation rental or tenant to home buyer program use by our Members. We charge cost plus 5%, which provides the reward for investment club member participation.

- **Corporate Contributor / Sponsorships** are used to fund events, incentives and rewards for Program Candidates.

- **Products and Services:** Primary profit generators, available to the general public online & off.

- **Referral Partners** earn a cash commission or 10% investment club dues credit for any registration, donation, sponsorship, or product/service that is earned because of a direct referral. Every time the company receives one dollar, the referral partner earns a 10% cut. Commissions are paid daily via paypal.

- **Profits:** 10% of profits will be used as a tithe, 10% for Founder and/or Executive Leadership Bonuses, 5% for staff and volunteer bonuses, 5% for business development / growing the company, 5% for savings, 5% will be donated to charity, and 60% will go to Ambassadors.

- **Ambassadors:** As a thank you for supporting this program, 60% of profits will be used to purchase gift cards that can be redeemed for cash or other prize packages, such as vacations, cruises, company ownership options, shopping sprees, etcetera. The size of your Ambassador reward will be based on your Membership level and will be split equitably among all Ambassadors.

Who Can Benefit?

Every individual, business owner, employee, not for profit, club, organization, or Christian organization in the US.

They are 9 ways that you can support our program. You are sure to find something that will resonate with your head, heart, and wallet.

Industry Specific Overview:

If you work in any of the following industries or provide support services to any of these industries, you should know that a significant portion of this program will be directly or indirectly tied to your industry.

Real estate sales, rental properties, property management, vacation rentals, tourism, hospitality, food & beverage, retail, mortgage brokers, lenders, and financial institutions.

Financial Services, Retirement Planning, Money Management, Credit Counseling, Wealth Management, and Insurance. Travel agencies, entertainment, fine arts, and philanthropic organizations.

I Have a Dream:

The American Dream is alive and well.

If that is true, why are so many Americans broke, miserable, and not living up to their God-given potential?

My name is Nancy Gaskins. I train INVESTORS.

I have a dream and a plan to help every household in America become more financially fit and significantly more prosperous over the next five years.

We INVEST in….

• Real Estate

• Small business ideas and start-ups,

• Everyday People in communities across America

I Have a Plan

This program is about increasing prosperity for every household in America; giving a hand UP, rather than a perpetual hand OUT.

Think of us as a mega-size nationwide investment club that every citizen can afford, and will be eager to participate, because every contributor is rewarded for their participation, no matter how large or small their effort.

We invest in real estate, business ideas, startups, and people. Working together, we can inspire, educate, reward, and transform lives in communities across America. The impact? World-wide, for generations.

9 Ways To Support This Program

1. Ambassador Memberships (Profit-sharing perk)

2. Investment Club Membership (Earn as you learn)

3. Vacation Club Membership (affordable vacation options)

4. Sponsorships (Advertising / Referrals)

5. Training Site Hosts (Private & Public Options)

6. Referral Partners (Earn cash fast)

7. Make a Donation (Rewards & Perks)

8. Wealth Builder Program Registration (Fast track tofinancial independence)

9. Purchase the book (PDF or paperback version)

Everyday families now have an affordable option to indirectly INVEST their money in something tangible and real; something that will truly make a difference in the lives of millions of families, and will impact generations to come.

Join me in my quest to make an investment in every household in America, giving each family the inspiration, tools and resources they need to become more prosperous as an individual, family, business, community and nation.

Nancy Gaskins, Founder
US Ambassadors for Prosperity

US AMBASSADORS

FOR PROSPERITY

Timeline

Phase 1:

Initial Campaign Goal: $ 10 Million

Wealth Builder Goal: $ 7.4 Billion

Referral Partnerships Kickoff

Ambassador Membership Drive

Prosperity Site Registrations

Sponsorships

Real Estate Investor Network Membership Drive

Retreat & Vacation Properties purchased

Residential Real Estate Investments purchased

Phase 2:

Applications Processed,

Trainers & Coaches Hired

Wealth Building Classes & Coaching Begin

Phase 3:

Community Investment Club Launch:

Small business startups and real estate investments for our Tenant to Home Buyer Program.

Phase 4:

Pay it forward, teach others to do the same.

Fundraiser Campaign Info

I currently have fundraiser campaigns listed on Kickstarter and Indigogo's Generosity.

Although these platforms are wonderful, please keep in mind that each platform has different rules regarding how the donations are handled and disbursed.

Some have significant fees attached, plus payment processor fees, which can be quite hefty, 10% or more. This really puts a dent in the amount of cash that is actually disbursed, and depending on which platform you choose, you may not have access to the cash until several weeks after the campaign has ended.

For those reasons, I have opted to provide a donation button on the website (www.iTrainInvestors.com) for those that wish to provide a cash GIFT of any amount to support the program. I will be able to access these funds immediately.

On the next page, I list the perks and rewards that are available for those who donate a gift of $5 or more.

I also have a list of other items that we need to support the program such as gift cards, office supplies, training materials, audios, books, gas cards, etcetera.

For those who are unable to participate or provide financial support, you can help by simply sharing this information with all your friends, family, neighbors and colleagues. If you are on social media, you can help this campaign go viral, achieving our goals in record time. Every penny and every dollar counts. Thank you!

Donor Perks and Rewards

Make a cash donation gift of $5 or more and receive exciting perks and rewards!

$5: FREE PDF version of the new book

$10: FREE PDF version of the new book PLUS and your name listed in the back as a Level 1 Contributor under your state.

$20: Receive all the perks above PLUS a certificate suitable for framing, and your name listed in the back as a Level 2 Contributor.

$50: Receive all the perks above PLUS a FREE autographed paperback copy of the new book, and your name listed as a Level 3 Ambassadors for Prosperity Hall of Fame Contributor.

$100: Receive all of the perks above PLUS get a personal INVITE to attend our Grand Opening Reception in Destin, FL (date TBA, planning for May 2017)

$125: Advertising & Promo - Business Owners / Non-profits / Clubs / Orgs

Receive all the perks above PLUS have your name, contact info and business logo listed in the back of the book as a Sponsor.

$500: Private Dinner Cruise - Destin, FL

Receive all of the perks listed above, PLUS receive an invitation to attend a private dinner cruise with live entertainment.

$1,000: Enjoy 2 nights of accommodations in fabulous Northwest Florida, home of sugar white sand, emerald green, crystal clear water. Perfect vacay getaway all year round! You will have up to 12 months to reserve your dates.

5 MORE Ways YOU Can Help

Challenge 1:
Spread the Love, Click Like & Share

Even if you are unable to make a donation or support the program financially, please consider sharing the information with others in your circles of influence.

There are an estimated 124.6 million families in the USA, 334 THOUSAND households in NW Florida. If each of them would contribute only $50, we could reach our goal to provide training for every household in America.

However, we both know that expecting 100% of our households to participate is an unrealistic expectation, which is why I am reaching out to as many people as possible to help me achieve this objective.

According to "Google," the average facebook user has an average of 338 friends. With your help, we can start a small spark that could go viral and help fund this program in just a matter of a few hours; not days, weeks, months or years. Will you help me by doing your part? Remember, every person that contributes and helps me achieve my goal will also be rewarded.

Challenge 2:
Accept the Challenge & Challenge Others

If each of you would accept the challenge yourself, and challenge 5 of your closest friends & family members and 5 colleagues to contribute $20 each, which would be $100 ($20 x 5), and ask them to do the same; i.e. challenge 5 of their closest friends and 5 colleagues... we could easily achieve our goal in less that a week and could start accepting applications and start the Wealth Builder Training program as soon as Spring 2017.

Challenge 3:
Refer qualified trainers, coaches and resources

Some of you may be interested in becoming a PAID trainer or coach for the program, or know of a colleague who would be qualified. Specifically, we need trainers and coaches for all personal finance topics, retirement planning, real estate investments, small business startups, entrepreneurship, and leadership development.

Challenge 4:
Donate Training Resources

We will be using top notch personal and professional development training programs that have a track record for success, such as the Dave Ramsey financial programs and John Maxwell leadership training programs, to name a few.

If you have personal and/or professional development books, dvds, audios, workbooks, courses, magazines or other materials that you would like to donate for our lending library, that would be fantastic. I will be posting a training resource wish list online for those of you who would be willing to make a purchase and donate to the lending library.

Challenge 5:
Donate rewards and incentives

Two of the four major pillars for success will be keeping each Ambassador inspired and moving forward in the program. We will do this by providing rewards and incentives each month and for completing certain financial milestones.

The rewards and incentives will start out small and get larger the more successful the Ambassadors and their teams become in achieving their financial goals and objectives.

If you would like to donate a gift card or certificate for the rewards program, I am suggesting restaurants, movie tickets, entertainment tickets, zoo, water park admission, Disney World or other similar amusement park tickets, vacation getaway lodging, gas cards, airline flights, retailer cards, hair salon, manicures, pedicures, spa, pontoon boat rentals, family canoe or camping trips, etcetera.

We are only limited by your imagination.

I am available to answer your questions by phone, email, online or at your place of business. My contact info can be found in the back of this book.

Non-profit Assistance

Clubs – Organizations – Churches - Christian Ministries

Does you club, organization or church have a mission to help people become more prosperous? If not, shouldn't you?

Perhaps you already provide something similar, but could use additional support to help more people.

Another option is you may want to provide this type of program as a reward, gift, scholarship, or incentive for your members, employees, clients, or volunteers.

Help us, help you!

1. Does your club, organization or church have a mission to help people in financial distress? Do you help with food, clothing, shelter, or utility bills? We have options to help you do more, for more people.

2. Does your organization already provide personal or professional development training opportunities? What about Dave Ramsey or other financial coaching, classes, or training with a track record for success? If so, we can help you reach more people by providing financial scholarships.

3. If your organization does not do either of these, perhaps you would consider becoming a training site whereby we bring in Trainers and Coaches to your facility each month or quarter and offer training to the public or you have the option to just provide them for your employees, staff, volunteers or members.

4. Could your organization use more exposure, more members, volunteers and support? Philanthropy and Community Service are two of the major cornerstones of the Wealth Builder Program. Every Ambassador is required to document volunteer hours with approved

organizations each month and when they are financially able, they will make financial contributions to causes in which they care about.

Your Organization will get a listing in our online directory AND a Profile page in our book, "Philanthropy 101: How to Create a Legacy that Endures." This book is mandatory reading, and all Members will be exposed to your Organization. Your organization will also have the opportunity to be interviewed on our online radio show, and you can also provide a short video commercial about your organization, if approved, can be uploaded to our youtube channel. Sponsors are also eligible to participate in community events throughout the nation.

Employee Benefit Program

Business Owners / Employers / Employment Agencies

Have you been looking for an affordable option to provide incentives and rewards for your staff, employees, suppliers, or vendors?

Providing a cost-effective way to help them take charge of their personal finances and become more prosperous is something that would be a win-win for both of you.

Did you know that money issues are a top reason cited for divorce, workplace absenteeism, low productivity, and stress; which leads to health problems. Alleviate this major stress factor, and you should see your employee start to shine more, their productivity and output increase, and your bottom line improve.

As an Employee benefit, this life enrichment gift would be something that will last a lifetime, and the impact will be felt for generations to come.

Consider becoming a Prosperity Training Site or providing this program as a gift or incentive for one of more employees who will attend classes and coaching sessions at a location in your community where we hold weekly and/or monthly training sessions.

Other options to consider would be to split the registration with the employee and have it taken out of their paycheck each cycle.

Sponsorship Opportunities

If you are looking for an affordable option to promote your business to a very large captive audience, or seeking ways to expand your reach nationwide, consider becoming a Sponsor.

Sponsors receive advertising and promotion in the back of all publications and events, as well as a business listing profile and link in our private online Shop Local Business Directory.

As a thank you for providing sponsorship, we will recommend that our Members purchase and use your products and services whenever possible.

Training Site Registrations

Consider becoming a Prosperity Training Site; a location where we hold our weekly or monthly training sessions. Sites may be designated as private (for your own private group), or community-based, which means it will be open to the public, and your group may also attend.

Public Sites: $365/Year

We handle all registrations and provide all materials and resources for those that we send to your site.

Private Sites: $125/Year plus Program Registration

Available for your own private group of employees, members, etcetera. We provide all materials and resources for a specified number of candidate registrations each year.

Real Estate Industry

Real Estate Investments will play a huge part in the success of this program. Real Estate will be the primary funding mechanism that I use to keep this program funded year after year.

The US Ambassadors for Prosperity Real Estate Investment portfolio will also serve as training for those who may be interested in using real estate investing as a way to build wealth.

If you are a Broker, Agent, Mortgage Lender Financial institution, Title Company or provide support services for real estate transactions, you can benefit from joining our team as a Sponsor.

a. Real Estate Investment Club:
Trading Soda For Real Estate – Earn as you Learn!

Dollar a Day Real Estate is a community investment club concept that was created and published back in 2009. This program has since been updated and will give everyday people affordable options to learn how to invest in real estate and grow their income without any of the hassles of buyers, sellers, or landlord duties...all for less than the price of one soda a day. No fine print, no red tape, no income or credit restrictions to participate.

b. Life's a Beach:
Help Me Provide Inspiration AND Hope

Each Wealth Builder Applicant will receive an all-expense paid RETREAT getaway. This retreat will be mandatory, not optional. It will be held in a beautiful beach location here in Northwest Florida or other sponsored locations where all distractions and stress factors will be removed.

This time will be spent creating and working on their new wealth building plan, with plenty of time to also relax and have fun.

Program goals, expectations, training materials, assignments and an assigned financial coach will be provided for each Applicant.

Each couple will leave with the tools and resources that they need to start implementing their plan.

c. Vacation Layaway Plan:

Based on the amount of funding we have available in our network, I will be investing in beach front, near beach front, and/or waterfront properties for the purpose of offering all-inclusive prepaid beach getaway vacation package to our members at cost, plus a small markup, if investors are involved in the transaction.

Obviously, if the goal is to provide accommodations and support services for 8.4 million families a year, I will need access to a **major network of lodging facilities** throughout the year who can provide accommodations; i.e. hotels, condos, vacation homes, resorts, and bed and breakfasts.

d. Vacation Club Deals:

There are 124. 6 million families in America. Every family will be invited to join our team, but not every Member will be participating in the Wealth Builders Program.

Every Member will, however, be strongly encouraged to take a mandatory vacation each year and our Vacation Club will provide incentives for them to achieve this objective.

If your business would like to offer our Members special deals on products and services, including accommodations and vacation packages, you must register as a Vacation Club Sponsor.

Special deals will be announced in our newsletter, email blasts and on our website each month.

e. Beach Getaway Prizes:

Other options will be to provide free 3-day and one week beach getaways for those who complete certain financial milestones.

f. Annual Conference:

At the end of each year, US Ambassadors for Prosperity, LLC will host an annual conference here in the region.

All Ambassadors, Sponsors, and Donors will be invited to attend. We will have training, vendors, and an awards banquet; where profit-sharing rewards and bonuses are announced and distributed.

We have great conference facilities and plenty of accommodations to handle a group of this size; again, adding another boost to our local economy.

If you are employed or involved in the real estate, restaurants, health, beauty & wellness, hospitality and/or tourist industry, including property management for resorts, hotels, condos, or beach homes, contact me immediately to see how we may can collaborate in 2017 and beyond.

Imagine what an extra 8 million families visiting our area a couple times per year could do for your business and your regional economy!

Emerald Coast Trivia:
How many visitors vacation along the Emerald Coast each year?

Answer: 4.5 million visitors

Wannabe Real Estate Investors

One of the best ways to build wealth is to invest in real estate.

Real estate Investments is a large, very important component of the US Ambassadors for Prosperity, LLC Wealth Building Program and we have an affordable option available for every household in America, no matter the size of your income or budget restraints.

Earn While You Learn!

If you are looking for an affordable opportunity to learn how to invest in real estate without any of the hassle of buyers, sellers, or landlord duties, consider joining our team as a Dollar a Day Real Estate Investor.

No red tape, no fine print, no experience, credit or income restrictions to participate. If you have at least $1 per day, $30 per month, $365 per year, which is less than the price of one soda a day, you can participate in our investment club; an earn as you learn training program for investors. There are different levels of membership available based on your budget.

Registration is Only $50 Per Year.

To encourage nationwide participation, I offer annual, semi-annual, monthly, and quarterly payment plan options for the Dues portion of your annual membership.

Dues are not billed until each community chapter has reached their membership goals. You will be notified at least 2 weeks ahead so you can have adequate time to budget accordingly.

Earn Cash Fast: I use a very simple, straight forward formula that is easy to understand and is a great deal for everyone involved.

I pay a $25 cash commission or $36.50 Dues Credit for every membership registration that I get from referrals during our Membership drive each year.

Start telling everyone you know and smile all the way to the bank! To help offset your annual dues, and help us achieve our membership goals in a timely manner, we will first apply all referral commissions towards your annual dues statement. Refer 10 people and your annual dues will be FREE!

Our pricing structure is cost, plus 5%, which is exactly what I charge our vacation club members, rental property tenants, or home buyers.

At the end of each year, all profits are rewarded back to our investment club members. You may opt to donate them back to the club to grow your account, or cash out.

Vacation Club Membership

One of the benefits available for Members is access to our private Vacation Club database which will contain special offers on vacation getaways, bucket list excursions, adventures, and special events.

Vacation at Cost:

You may vacation in any of our vacation properties for cost plus 5%; which is the fee our real estate investment club members earn each year for providing our investment capital.

Group Savings:

Each month Vacation Club Sponsors will offer special perks, incentives and discounts exclusive to our members. Members will be polled so that we are able to plan exciting vacation packages, bucket list excursions and experiences. We will pass the savings along to our Members.

The Bottom Line…

If YOU don't join our team, chances are… your family, friends, colleagues, and neighbors will be the ones enjoying all the perks, benefits, and rewards instead of you.

If your business doesn't provide products and services for all these people, your competitors will.

If your region won't host these 8.4 million customers each year, another region will. Don't let this opportunity slide by.

Part 2
The Plan

1. Introduction

US Ambassadors for Prosperity, LLC is a citizen-led, entrepreneurial initiative that provides incentives and rewards to families who are committed to living a life of excellence in both their personal and professional lives; always striving to improve their own life, and the life of others.

Our primary objectives are to eradicate poverty and the entitlement mindsets that plague America day in and day. Our secondary focus is to help families become more prosperous, year after year.

For those on welfare, we truly want to help you succeed. We want YOU to be the one; perhaps the first one in your family for many generations back, to BREAK the poverty cycle and eliminate your dependency on government assistance programs.

We want you to thrive and become a productive member of society. When that happens, a ripple effect begins to take place. Not only does your immediate family benefit, but your extended family, friends, co-workers, neighborhood, community, region, state and nation benefits as well.

You may not be on government assistance. You may have a job and a great income, but you know in your heart that you are not living up to your full potential.

You'd love the opportunity to get on track to accomplish more in one year than most will accomplish in a lifetime. You are ready for opportunity and willing to do what it takes to get your life on the fast track to being the life you were meant to live.

Others may be perpetrating a fraud; on the outside, you have all the signs of success, but your financial report card would tell a different story.

You live paycheck to paycheck, leveraged to the hilt in debt, and you spend money like you have a money tree in your back yard.

You spend your money on things that are not really assets, although you may convince yourself otherwise. (Think jewelry, electronic gadgets, shoes, name brand clothes, handbags.) If you lost your job, you would probably be bankrupt in a few short months, if even that long.

The program is fueled and funded by citizens across America who are fed up with themselves, fed up with each other, and certainly fed up with our government wasting our hard-earned tax dollars.

INVESTING in our people is the absolute best way to provide a hand UP; which is much better than a perpetual hand OUT…any day of the week.

2. Accountability

No red tape, No BS....and full disclosure. We track everything. We are serious about helping you achieve and succeed. You will be respected always, and will demand the same in return.

We will not blow smoke, we will not tell you what you want to hear. We will tell you the truth and sometimes the truth will sting and won't feel very good. This is how we grow and become better.

We will be working hard to identify and change bad, destructive mindsets and habits, replacing them with ones that are more conducive to you achieving your dreams.

We love to celebrate! We will enjoy celebrating and recognizing you for your achievements, no matter how big or small. Keep in mind, you are also an investment, which means you will be expected to do your part. We will not ask you to do anything unless we feel it is in YOUR best interest to do so.

You can expect friendly competitions designed to keep you inspired and motivated to keep pressing forward, achieving your milestones, always keeping your eyes on the end objective. Financial freedom, living the life of your dreams, your version of the American Dream.

3. Background

One of the problems with many government programs is they don't fix the problem. They provide a "band aid" that will temporarily relieve the symptom of being broke.

A famous Chinese proverb says, "feed a man a fish, feed him a day; teach a man to fish, feed him for a lifetime."

Government programs focus on the first part, which leads to "dependency." My goal for this program is to provide the second part, which will lead to "independence."

Funding:

Every year, WE THE PEOPLE are forced to provide more tax dollars to fund 13 separate welfare programs, each independent of the other. I have no idea of how many other not for profit organizations or institutions that are being funded to work on this issue. One thing I do know is that the numbers are not getting any smaller.

The left hand is not talking to the right, so to speak, which leads to tons of red tape, duplication of effort, no real accountability and in the business world we call this a "perpetual" money pit. In 2015, our government was spending $712 BILLION dollars per year fighting poverty. Once it's spent, we never get it back.

The Proposal:

I have a much better idea. I propose that WE THE PEOPLE build a "cash machine" that will generate a source of perpetual income to fund this program.

This means that if done correctly, we could fund this program once, and it will self-fund every year thereafter.

Currently, **21.3 million** families are on SNAP (Supplemental Nutrition Assistance Program), which most of us know as the "food stamp" program.

SNAP is only one of the thirteen programs aimed at poverty. There are 3.6 million SNAP participants in the state of Florida, and 34,278 households who are participating in Florida Congressional District One.

The Prosperity Plan: The plan is to raise enough initial funding to provide 4.2 million families with FREE wealth building classes and coaching each year. These families will in turn, pay it forward and will pay for 4.2 million more families. In year 2, we will be able to fund our scheduled 4.2 million families PLUS 4.2 million MORE families due to the pay it forward concept. That's a total of **8.4 million** families trained in year two.

For icing on the cake, 5% of our profits each year goes towards business development, which means more products, services, more cash available to spend on helping more families.

We have an annual Membership Drive each year for Ambassador Memberships. This money is invested in real estate and the income generated from each property is used to fund the program. Again, more funding to provide more wealth building training for more families.

Snowball Effect:

It won't take long for this small snowball to turn into a massive avalanche. Our initial funding provides a steady stream of income to provide training for 4.2 million per year. The pay it forward doubles our investment, and the annual membership drive and profit sharing drives our investment capital up even higher. In layman terms, this means that in a very short period of time, we can literally have enough funding available to provide wealth building training for every household in America!

This plan can work if everyone will pitch in and help lighten the load. All we need is enough funding to start the snowball rolling…we will let momentum take care of the rest! Won't you join us today and help us provide FREE Wealth Building Classes to EVERY household in America? Isn't YOUR family worth it?

4. The Dream

Everyday families will have an affordable option to INVEST their money in something that will truly make a difference in the lives of millions of families, and will impact generations to come.

Imagine the excitement and economic impact in small communities across America when unemployed and under-employed families start working again...in jobs they LOVE.

Those with dreams of owning and operating their own business will have access to affordable options that will help those dreams come to pass. Those who have great business ideas will be PAID to do what they do best...generate business ideas.

Families who desire to own their very own slice of paradise will have the tools and resources that will enable them to achieve the dream of home ownership. Many will dream and achieve the goal of becoming completely mortgage free. Imagine that! Yes, it's possible.

All Ambassadors will have a vested interest in the success of all other Ambassadors. For that reason, we all should be more inclined to help fellow members find suitable employment.

When someone asks us for a referral or recommendation; our first response should be to look in our Ambassador Directory and refer a fellow Ambassador. If given a choice, always try to support our fellow Ambassadors.

When Ambassadors fund a new project, that business should clearly be on every Ambassador's radar. We want that new business to succeed. Since we have a vested interest, we will demand and expect excellence from the business owner, employees, staff, suppliers...on down the food chain.

If we see something out of line, we will be sure to help make sure that issue is brought to the business owner's attention so that it can be corrected asap.

Our mission is to help every Ambassador in our Network to become more successful. When you succeed, we all celebrate. When you fail, we are there to help you get back up and start again.

Making a World of Difference:

THIS program is created to help fuel and fund the American Dream. I expect the impact will be like an economic atomic bomb going off in the USA, which by the ripple effect, will spread from family member to family member, to neighbors, across neighborhoods, communities, states, our nation, to the rest of the world.

Target Markets

1. US Citizens on Government Assistance Programs

2. Unemployed Citizens

3. Underemployed Citizens: Those who are working beneath your potential, those that are working part-time, that desire to be working full time.

4. Every household in America

5. Those word-wide who embrace our philosophies and desire to create the same outcomes for their lives.

5. Small Business Owners

Of all people, YOU understand that entrepreneurship is the backbone of our country. Our government is a behemoth, full of red tape and bureaucracy. Entrepreneurs know how to get things done...better, faster, cheaper.

That's why it makes such perfect sense that WE entrepreneurs take on this challenge to eradicate poverty and help people rise and overcome the entitlement philosophy that plagues America. Together we can empower and equip the people of our nation for PROSPERITY.

As a Founding Ambassadors for Prosperity Member, you will be helping to fuel and fund the American Dream. With your help, WE can transform our nation, along with making a world of difference in the lives of others, save tax dollars, and stimulate our economy.

If you like the sound having access to an additional income stream, that has the potential to increase year after year, into perpetuity, you owe it to yourself and your family to join us in our quest to help jump start this program.

If you'd love to share you experience, skills set and education; consider becoming an Entrepreneurship trainer, mentor, or coach. Other options include sitting on the Executive Board and Leading Mastermind Teams.

6. Real Estate Brokers, Agents & Investors

Whath would the commissions be on $7.4 Billion dollars' worth of real estate in 2017? Would you like to have a piece of the action?

US Ambassadors for Prosperity will be using real estate investments as a major tool to help eradicate poverty in the US.

Memberships, Sponsorships, and Donations are used to purchase real estate investments. The rental income generated from each property will provide the funding necessary to pay all expenses each year, including the Wealth Building Training and Coaching.

This is a great way to guarantee funding year after year instead of a onetime shot where all the funding is spent and there is no more available to replace it.

Tenant to Home Buyer Program:

Our goal is to help 4.2 million families each year get on the fact track to financial success and prosperity. One of the major dreams and financial milestones for many families is being able to afford a home of their own.

Ambassadors will have options to choose one of our properties for rental purposes until they are financially able to transition up to the next stage, where they will be preparing to buy their own home.

To become a Sponsor, goto:
www.USAmbassadorsForProsperity.com.

7. Mortgage Brokers & Agents

Do you ever have mortgage applicants that get down to the wire and something happens to prevent the closing?

It may not be anything major. Sometimes, the problem can be resolved in a couple of weeks and all that is needed is to push out the closing date.

However, sometimes, the closing must be put off for a longer period, which means most Applicants will lose out on the home of their dreams because the Seller can't wait that long.

We want to provide an interim solution for you and these families. Our Dollar a Day Real Estate community investment club will be able to provide interim financing and personal finance coaching and accountability for your Client.

We will purchase the home on their behalf and they will be able to move in as scheduled. Once they are able to qualify for a mortgage, we will automatically recycle them back to your office for a traditional mortgage.

To become a Sponsor, goto:

www.USAmbassadorsForProsperity.com.

8. Banking & Financial Institutions

Contact *Nancy.Gaskins@operationHSH.com* to learn how your institution can benefit from teaming up with US Ambassadors for Prosperity to provide your banking customers and clients Wealth Building Training and Coaching.

To become a Sponsor, goto:

www.USAmbassadorsForProsperity.com.

9. Opportunity of a Lifetime?

U S Ambassadors for Prosperity is a Florida Limited Liability Company.

Instead of Shareholders who have stock options in a corporation, an LLC has "owners," or "Members."

At the end of each fiscal year, we have a celebration and provide rewards and incentives to all those who have helped us achieve our goals for the year.

One of the benefits of being a **Founding Member** is that you have the option to redeem your rewards toward becoming shareholders of the company.

Some of you may desire become more actively involved by sitting on our Executive Board of Directors and help guide the company towards the future.

If you are looking for opportunities with GREAT potential; this might be the one in which you might regret passing by.

10. Show Me The Money!

The most pressing issue to address FIRST is our finances. **To become more prosperous**, you must have access to enough cash to survive, spend, save, invest, and give away.

We have such a significant percentage of our people that are on government assistance programs, are under-employed, or unemployed. That means there is a big cash shortage.

These families have barely enough cash to survive, which makes it impossible to do anything in the other four categories.

Did you know that you can be broke on an income of $10 thousand a month? You could be more "wealthy," than the one with the great income.

The difference is whether you let your money determine where it is going, or whether you tell your money where to go; in other words, how you handle your finances, no matter the amount of the income will determine the outcome of your financial future.

There are too many people that have the *"keeping up with the Jones"* syndrome. They always have the finest of everything, the big house, the fine cars, the bags, and the shoes; but…they have no true wealth.

They are leveraged to the hilt with debt and no equity. They are perpetrating a fraud and most people don't know the difference. You will learn to spot those people. If this describes you, it's okay. Recognizing you have a problem is the first step to finding a solution.

Others struggle with mounds of debt, credit issues, have very little, if any emergency savings net, and we all know there will be one. We don't know when; but we do know it's coming, and most won't be prepared.

The typical American will attest that there always seems to be "too much month left," at the end of their money. More often than not, families say they are not on track to meet their retirement goals. Many retirees are forced to get part-time jobs that they hate, just to supplement their incomes.

Money problems can cause all kinds of problems, most notably stress and health-related issues. Relationships suffer. Money issues are one of the top items cited for divorce. Everyone around you suffers, and your performance at work will also suffer, which many times leads to even more of a financial emergency if you lose your job without an adequate emergency savings plan.

For those who say that "money isn't everything," how about trying to live without it for a month or two? I bet your viewpoint would change.

It tickles me to hear people say that, *"money is the root of all evil."* I think "LACK" OF money is the culprit. Don't think so? Wait until you have a dire financial emergency and see how many awful schemes roll around in your mind that would help you solve the crises.

One of my all-time favorites is a quote from Mame: *"money isn't everything, but it sure makes miserable a lot more tolerable!"*

The Bottom Line...

If we all want to be more prosperous, the first step is to get our financial house in order.

Once that is done, STEP TWO is when you will have extra so that you can start investing your money and making it work for you.

One day, your money will be working so hard for you that you will no longer be required to go punch the dreaded time clock each day, and you can fire your boss if you want to.

That is the day that you will have achieved true financial independence!

11. How Much Funding Do We Need?

With an investment of $5.4 BILLION dollars, we can provide the Prosperity Wealth Building Program to every family who is currently receiving food stamps, which, according to the USDA website, is currently 21.3 million families.

My plan is to train a minimum of 4.26 million families per year, for the next five years. At that point, program funding will totally be on autopilot, providing training and investment opportunities to any household in America who desires to learn how to become more prosperous.

A successful outcome of this program will mean that every able-bodied person that wants to work will be working, earning, saving, and investing.

New business ideas will be generated and small business startups will be launched in cities across America.

Friends, neighbors and co-workers will be the first ones to notice the small changes in our Ambassador's attitude and lifestyle.

Small business owners in communities across America will start experiencing a surge in sales and increase in profitability.

People who work at their full potential will earn at their full potential, which means you will have money to spend, save, invest and give away!

All those "causes," you wished you could afford to support? As an Ambassador, you will have the funding established to just write a check when the opportunity presents itself.

Pay It Forward

The pay it forward concept is a critical component for our program to continue to be funded year after year so we can achieve our long-term goals. Every Ambassador, without exception will be required to sponsor a family, just as they have been sponsored.

"Paying it forward" enables us to do the same for other Ambassadors, on a first-come, first serve basis, based on funding availability in the Network.

Each of us have limited knowledge. We have our strong suits and weaknesses. We struggle in some areas of our finances, but thrive in others. It's imperative that we all are all working from the same page, have a rock-solid financial foundation in place that will enable us to meet our future financial goals and objectives.

IMPOSSIBLE?

At first glance, for most Americans, **$5.4 billion dollars** probably seems a completely outrageous amount of money. Most of you reading this would think this would be an impossible amount of cash to have to raise in such a short time period, but hear me out….

Remember, our government is currently spending **$712 BILLION per year** on 13 different Welfare Programs, not including Medicaid, which is the insurance program for those with low income. If something is not done, this money pit will just continue indefinitely. We need every able-bodied American fully-employed, being a productive member of society. We need everyone to be at the top of their game, using all their gifts and talents, thriving. We need the extra money to be spent on reducing our deficit, not on welfare benefits.

*** Let's Break It Down ***

Current Government Spending:

124.6 million household in the USA

$712 billion dollars

$5,714.29 Per Household EVERY year

Our Program:

$5.4 Billion to Launch & Implement

$ 43.34 Per Household ONE TIME

	100 % HHs	50% HHs	25% HHs	10% HHs
HH	124,600,000	62,300,000	31,150,000	12,460,000
Funding	5,400,000,000	5,400,000,000	5,400,000,000	5,400,000,000
Cost / HH	$ 43.34	$ 86.68	$ 173.35	$ 433.39
Monthly	$ 3.61	$ 7.22	$ 14.45	$ 36.12
Weekly	$ 0.83	$ 1.67	$ 3.33	$ 8.33
Daily	$ 0.12	$ 0.24	$ 0.47	$ 1.19

➤How to read this chart:

If 100% of households would donate $43.34 one time; we could fund this program. Breaking it down, that equates to $3.61 per month, $0.83 per week, and $0.12 per day.

➤Putting the Numbers In Perspective:

Compare this to the current government spending of $5,714 per household per year, $476.16 per month, $109.88 per week, and $15.65 per day, INDEFINATELY.

You can also view this program as an opportunity to save $712 billion dollars a year in tax dollars, which equates to a savings of $5,714.29 per household.

What could YOU do with an extra $5 grand per year? That would pay for one fantastic family vacation, yes?

➤Can You See The Forest Or Just the Trees?

$5.4 billion is just a very small price to pay to reap the rewards and benefits that this program will provide.

I think anyone with half a brain is able to understand the significance of a small investment, from WE THE PEOPLE, up front.

That ONE TIME ONLY small investment will pay huge dividends in the years to come. The financial programs that we will be using have an unbelievable track record for getting amazing results, in just a short 90-days. I can't imagine how exciting one year from today will be like for our Ambassador family.

12. The Challenge

The biggest challenge that I face is "getting the word out," to the masses.

As you can see in the numbers on the previous pages, breaking it down shows that this can easily be achieved. Most people waste more money each month than what this program would take to properly fund.

There are some people who have more cash available to participate. Some will be able to contribute weekly, monthly, while others only once a year. Every dollar counts. Every penny matters.

Annual Fundraiser Campaign:

I have absolutely no desire to be forced to launch fundraiser campaigns month after month, year after year. My goal is to do it ONE TIME, invest those proceeds and use the income generated to fund the program month after month, year after year, into perpetuity.

Each year we will conduct a membership drive and will know exactly how much cash we have available to invest, and how many families we can accept into the program. The rest of the time our focus can be on more ways to help our Ambassador families become more prosperous.

How YOU Can Help

Let's work together in communities across America to **help me spread the word**. Even if you are unable to donate, become an Ambassador or Sponsor, you can help by simply sharing this info with everyone in your network. Hopefully, it will catch on like wildfire and go viral. Think of those in your network who could benefit. Think of those you know that work for newspapers, magazine, news, television stations, radio, church, associations, clubs, not for profit organizations.

Remember, every household, business, organization, and non-profit is eligible to participate. The program can benefit every citizen of this country and beyond our border. This is not hype; this is the true potential.

13. Earn Cash Fast

The focus of this program is helping our people become more prosperous, which should appeal to most everyone, including yourself. It's very easy to become a Referral Partner.

1. Click on the Referral Partner registration link: *www.USAmbassadorsForProsperity.org*

2. I will assign you an affiliate link to use to track your referrals,

3. You may download and print marketing materials direct from the website, or you can purchase them from me at wholesale cost. I will order in bulk each week, based on demand.

4. Every time I receive a membership, sponsorship, book purchase or donation based on your efforts, you will receive a 10% cash commission, paid DAILY.

This is not a sales job; put a public relations one. Your objective is to invite as many people as possible to REVIEW the program. It can be as easy as sending a text, forwarding an email, or sharing a post on your wall through social media.

For others, you may prefer a face to face invitation. Hand out postcard invitations to everyone you see or you may want to plan a more targeted approach and go after a certain target market.

Another option is to purchase the From Welfare to Faring Well book online and share it with those you know. It's a short read that explains everything. The Prosperity Training Program is available nationwide, but Ambassadorship Membership and Sponsorship opportunities is world-wide. The more people we have participating, the more funding we will have available in our Ambassador Network.

To sign up to become a referral partner, click here: *www.USAmbassadorsForProsperity.org*

14. Ambassador Rewards

There are many options to support this program. You can make a donation of any amount, purchase a book, become a Sponsor or Ambassador.

Ambassadors are eligible to receive incentives and rewards each year based on how well our organization meets its objectives. This gives everyone a vested interest in helping us all become more prosperous throughout the year.

As a thank you for helping me achieve MY dream of helping others, at the end of each fiscal year, I will host an annual party where we will recognize and reward our Founding Ambassadors, Ambassadors, Staff and Volunteers.

Profit Breakdown and Spending Categories

As you will see in the breakdown below. We will practice what we preach when it comes to handling our finances. Our expenses will be paid on time, we will not incur debt, and we will be generous to all those who help us succeed.

10% of profits will be used as a tithe, 10% for Founder and/or Executive Leadership Bonuses, 5% for staff and volunteer bonuses, 5% for business development / growing the company, 5% for savings, 5% will be donated to charity, and 60% will go to Ambassadors.

60% will be used to purchase gift cards that can be redeemed for cash or other prize packages, such as vacations, cruises, company ownership options, shopping sprees, etcetera.

The size of your Ambassador reward will be based on your Membership level and will be split equitably among all Ambassadors.

15. It's Time to Take Action

Chapters are now forming in communities across America. Are you ready to be part of something that is bigger than yourself?

Imagine, something that we do THIS YEAR will have a major impact on the personal, professional, and financial lives of families, for generations to come.

Help eradicate poverty and promote prosperity in America.

Register as a US Ambassador for Prosperity today!

To Register:

1. *www.USAmbassadorsForProsperity.com*

2. Click on any date

3. Choose which level of Ambassadorship or Sponsorship you wish to join

4. You will receive a welcome email upon registration.

16. Life Enrichment Topics

1. Strategic Life Planning
2. Personal Finance
3. Wealth Building
4. Entrepreneurship 101
5. Health, Fitness & Nutrition
6. Leadership & Management Development
7. Career Advancement Strategies
8. Higher Education Opportunities
9. Networking
10. Building Better Relationships
11. Communication
12. Anger Management / Conflict Resolution
13. Self-esteem and Assertiveness
14. Stress Management
15. Critical Thinking & Problem Solving
16. How to Dress For Success
17. Beauty & Fashion
18. Christianity
19. Civics & Patriotism
20. Community Service

17. Five Pillars For Success

- Inspire
- Educate
- Reward
- Transform
- Pay it Forward

Inspire

We all need inspiration and something to look forward to. Many times, life has kicked us around so much that we get discouraged and can't see the forest for the trees.

How long has it been since you have had a REAL vacation? If you live here in Northwest Florida at the beach, how long has it been since you played "tourist," and enjoyed your "staycation" home? You live here and are probably so busy that chances are, you don't take much time to just sit and enjoy where you live. It truly is paradise.

Since the people we hang around the most, have the most influence, perhaps you could use an infusion of new, optimistic friends who are ambitious, competitive, can inspire you, encourage you, hold you accountable, as in "calling you out," when you need it, and challenge you to reach higher than you have ever gone before.

This program will help remove the negative and toxic people from your life.

Your physical surroundings make a huge difference in how you view life. It's not so much about having the most money or expensive "things," to be inspirational, although that can be inspirational for some. *Your daily surroundings can be inspiring or they can drag you down.*

My job is to help you identify the things, people, places and things that inspire you the most and help you bring more of that into your daily life.

To set the stage and get your mind "right," you and a small team of other Applicants will join me on a FREE, two day, all-expense paid, retreat, in luxury accommodations. You will leave inspired, equipped and empowered to go conquer the world!

Everyone has a different viewpoint on what they consider to be their version of "living the American Dream." My best definition that I think we all can agree to would be the one I have chosen as our Mission Statement:

Create a lifestyle where I will have enough money, time, health and fitness to do what I want, when I want, with those that mean the most.

Educate

Education can come in many forms; i.e. formal, informal, from your experience, and the experience of others.

Have you ever heard the saying, "you don't know what you don't know? There's a strong possibility that you probably don't know as much as you think you do.

The younger you are, the more you have to learn. Trust me, the older you get, the wiser your parents and grandparents will become. Things you think are "major," may not be as "major," as you think.

Everything you know is based on the lenses of YOUR life and those in your circle of influence. If you have never stepped foot outside your county, city, state or nation; it's a fair assumption that you probably have a very narrow perspective of the world, in general.

If you haven't failed, you haven't learned. As long as you are not repeating the same mistakes, the more times you fail, the closer you are to attaining that big WIN you are seeking.

The Value of Advice: Many mistakes that are made, could have easily been prevented if we had not taken advice from the <u>wrong people.</u>

Who are the most common culprits who dole out the most bad or misguided advice? <u>Family and friends.</u> They mean well, of course.

Don't think so? Why do people continue to take advice about money from people who don't have any? How about the marriage counselors who have had 3 failed marriages and is involved in an extramarital affair right now?

One of my favorites is people who have never had children, giving parental advice. Isn't it comical to hear a doctor tell someone they need to quit smoking, drinking and lose weight when he does the exact same thing?

Bottom line: be sure your source is credible and has a track record for success, not failure. That means they *"walk the walk,"* and *"talk the talk."*

Another issue is that we tend to get lazy, not do our due diligence and research properly or we think we don't have time and so we just don't research at all.

We make life altering decisions and snap judgments without blinking an eye. Some of these decisions will change the trajectory of your life forever; some not as much.

You must strive become a better problem solver, make better decisions, and when you do, you will see your life begin to make course corrections in the direction in which you had planned.

Masterminds / Coaches: The world's greatest athletes, entertainers, business moguls, and anyone worth their salt can tell you the value of having a mastermind group, mentor, accountability partner, and coach that they know, like, respect and trust.

Their job is not to be your friend. Their job is to help you be BETTER. They see things you don't. They see your potential and your weaknesses. Whatever skill or goal you have for your life, you should find someone who has already "been there, done that," and learn from them.

By tapping into their experience, knowledge, skills set, instincts, and following their advice… you can **reach farther, faster**. Instead of learning personally from the "school of hard knocks," you can learn from someone else's hard knocks, which can save you tons of heartache, grief, time and money.

Higher or HIRE Education: I love learning. I am a self-professed personal and professional development junkie. I have a fabulous library in my home filled with great books; most of them are books that help me be BETTER in all areas of my life.

I read all the time, research online, go to training, seminars, retreats and conferences every chance I get, and I have several business degrees.

Be careful here. Don't go just to go. The objective is to learn something that you can either apply to your personal or professional life. Many make the mistake of getting all the training, but when they go home, what they have learned fails to get implemented. When this happens, you have just really wasted time and money.

I challenge you to make it a point to focus on what you are learning, find at least ONE SOLID NUGGET that you can immediately apply to your life. Keep track. This will help you keep track of what's working and what is not working.

It's sad to me that I know people who have never picked up a book since they left high school. Books are so magical; they can take you to places you have never been before, give you access to wonderful experiences through the eyes of the characters in a story, inspire you, give you advice, teach you lessons, make you think, laugh, and cry.

Although I love my library and love having my hands wrapped around a physical book, I love having access to worldwide knowledge via the internet and millions of books and audiobooks at my fingertips.

Point to Ponder

I don't care if my plumber went to college and has his Ph.D. I will gladly pay him top dollar to come fix my problem. He has a specialized trade, specialized skill set, and doesn't "need," a degree to be successful.

You may not need one either. If you are contemplating higher education, be sure to ask yourself the real reason that you desire to go. I love the classroom setting, I do well on tests. Others may not.

Online classes are very popular now, but as a former Dean of Business and Director of Education, I really worry about the quality of those classes. Be sure to do your due diligence when deciding upon an academic program from any institution.

Some of you may be saying that you can't afford to go, or don't have time to go to college right now. So what? I used to go to the college bookstore and buy used textbooks and take them home to read. I'd go to the library and check out books and audio cassettes that helped me get ahead in life and at work. With advancements in technology today, "knowledge" is just one google search away. The key is to identify the key skill sets that will help you get from where you are, to where you want to be.

So many people complain about the job market right now. It's an excuse and smoke screen for the truth. What that really means is that the market is not in need of your specific skill sets right now.

You can mope around complaining until the cows come home, but the fact remains…YOU have a problem that needs to be solved.

There are several options from which you can choose to solve your dilemma, but one in which you can never go wrong: **Do whatever it takes to expand your HIRE job skill sets**. Find out what the market is demanding and give it to them.

This program is designed to be flexible and offer Applicants training, coaching, mentoring, along with accountability procedures that will help make you well-rounded and BETTER… in every aspect of your life, not just your finances.

Rewards & Incentives:

One of my major pet peeves is when teachers, coaches, parents, or employers give out rewards that are not earned. Participation trophies, certificates, you get my drift. All that does is devalue the prize and it becomes just a worthless piece of paper boxed up in the attic somewhere.

Sometimes, in cases like the government welfare system, incentives have negative and unintended consequences. That system is designed (intentionally or not) to keep people totally dependent upon the government.

After a while, this dependency will typically show up in other areas of your life and self-sabotaging will begin. Your negative self-talk will lower your self-esteem and confidence, you will start having a bad attitude and negative outlook regarding every area of your life, and start cutting corners, justifying everything because life is so unfair and after all, "you deserve it."

There is nothing more exciting than setting a big goal, working hard and achieving it; except for maybe a REWARD and RECOGNITION for your achievement. We all enjoy praise and recognition for our efforts, when it has been truly EARNED.

The problem with big bodacious goals is that if you don't set up some mini-goals and celebrate those milestone achievements, you might get frustrated and give up altogether because you are not seeing instantaneous results. If you enjoy little successes along the way, you will stay motivated and your excitement will be contagious and spread to everyone around you! You will now be inspiring others to follow suit!

This program is designed specifically to give Applicants enough incentives and milestone rewards that you will be inspired to do whatever it takes to get your family off government assistance programs, living and thriving on your own accord.

18. Pay it Forward

A common problem with people that are GIVEN something for "nothing," is they don't appreciate what they are given.

There are a few exceptions to the rule, but based on my own personal experience, if they have "no skin in the game," so to speak, they really don't have much of an incentive to do their very best.

In fact, if not careful they will become so accustomed to getting something for nothing that they will begin to "expect," something for nothing. This is called an "entitlement," mentality, and one of main reasons, in my humble opinion, that are country is in such bad shape.

This program is based on every participant to have some "skin," in the game.

You must be a registered Ambassador to participate in the free Wealth Building Program. If you don't complete a module or assignment, you will be required to pay a penalty.

Fostering good citizenship is a major component of this program, and I realize that most families, especially in the beginning, won't have much CASH to spend on philanthropy, so, instead, you will be required to volunteer and log community service hours each month.

If you fail to complete this assignment each month, you will be penalized and required to make a cash donation in lieu of your volunteer hour shortage.

My hope is that you will be introduced to many wonderful organizations in your community and realize how important volunteers and donations are for them to survive.

I further hope that you will find a few that you really love and will continue volunteering and donating your hard-earned cash to these worthwhile charities long after you complete this program.

There are at least **21.3 million households** who are eligible for our services. YOU are here because someone wanted to help make a difference in your life.

This program is not free. You will be expected to pay the same courtesy, by **sponsoring another family** once you finish the program, or become financially able, whichever comes first. Our goal is to keep this program going year after year through the kindness and generosity of our "*pay it forward*," sponsors.

19. Implementation Plan

- •Secure Funding
- •Lay the Groundwork
- •Launch

1. Ambassador Membership Drive Kickoff - donations, sponsorships and annual membership fees will be used to provide start-up capital and operating expenses.

2. Submit cash offers for real estate investment properties that will be used to (a) provide inspiration and reward members for achieving certain milestones, and (b) provide a perpetual stream of income that will help offset the costs to keep the program funded year after year.

3. Purchase and place the supporting assets and supplies for each property.

4. Vet applications and select our first cohort of candidates.

5. Schedule and advertise an open house reception for sponsors & program candidates.

6. Financial Classes Begin

7. Survey Ambassadors for top Benefit & Training Topics

8. Hire a team of professional coaches that will develop and provide a personal & professional development training series, incentive & rewards program, accountability and individual and group coaching sessions for our members.

9. Launch a members-only website that will serve as a membership directory and hub for all personal and professional development training, discussion forums, coaching sessions, employment and business opportunities,

online store, calendar of events, competitions, newsletter, and magazine.

10. Launch podcast, book series, newsletter, and magazine

11. Launch community investment clubs to fund small business startup grants and real estate investments for the Tenant to Home Buyer Program.

What's Next?

It's time to join our team!

1. Make a donation, join our team as an Ambassador, Wealth Building Candidate, Coach/Trainer, or Sponsor.

2. Keep up with the latest news on our facebook page: USAmbassadorsForProsperity, or visit our website at *www.iTrainInvestors.com*.

20. Marketing and Publicity

You may download and print all the material I make available online for this purpose. You are only allowed to use authorized artwork.

I will be making a bulk order each week, based on demand, and will pass the savings along to you; which means you can purchase the pieces at wholesale cost, and have smaller quantities.

Visit the website *www.iTrainInvestors.com* to see the latest marketing and promotional materials available.

Introducing
Nancy S. Gaskins

Introducing Serial Entrepreneur Nancy S. Gaskins, a Speaker, Author, Radio Talk Show Host, and Investor that specializes in Entrepreneurship, Real Estate Investing and Wealth Building.

Nancy invests in people, real estate, small business startups, clubs, organizations and Christian-based ministries.

Nancy Gaskins has over 20 years of Sales, Marketing, and Senior Level Management experience. Ms. Gaskins is a former Corporate Controller, Conference Event Planner, Director of Education, Dean, College Professor of Business. As a proud US Army spouse of 23+ years, she has lived and worked around the globe in a variety of industries.

Ms. Gaskins received the President's Volunteer Service Award for her lifetime commitment to Community Service, the Heroine of the Infantryman's Shield of Sparta for her work supporting the Infantry Branch of the US Army, as well as numerous awards and recognition for her years of community service.

Nancy is the founder of US Ambassadors for Prosperity; a 5-year plan to eradicate poverty in the US by providing free wealth building and entrepreneurship classes and coaching to every household in America.

Nancy is available for the following:

- Key Notes and Guest Speaker for Seminars/Workshops/Conferences

- Advisory or Executive Boards

- Training & Development Facilitator

- Business Consulting

- Coaching, and Strategic Planning

Part 3
SPONSORS

Thank you to all the generous Donors, Sponsors, Corporate Contributors, Training Site Hosts, Investors, Members and Ambassadors who contributed your time, money, or other resources to make this program possible.

I encourage you to do business with, and refer others to those individuals, businesses and organizations that have supported our efforts.

Donors by State

EXAMPLE:

Florida

Gaskins, Rob & Nancy

Training Site Hosts

EXAMPLE:

Florida

US Ambassadors for Prosperity, LLC
Navarre, FL 2566
www.iTrainInvestors.com

Sponsors

EXAMPLE:

Florida

US Ambassadors for Prosperity, LLC
Navarre, FL 2566
www.iTrainInvestors.com

www.ingramcontent.com/pod-product-compliance
Lightning Source LLC
Chambersburg PA
CBHW051729170526
45167CB00002B/856